BIG: A "God-Sized Vision" for Your Church

An Uncomplicated Approach to Defining and Declaring a Compelling Vision for Your Church

Stan J. Tharp, D.Min.

TABLE OF CONTENTS

Introduction: How This Book Can Help Your Church

Have you ever wondered why some churches flourish and some churches struggle? I've been in full time "church work" since 1979 and I definitely have. Adding to this quandary, if you attend any of the leadership conferences or church growth seminars popular today, concepts often either seem out of reach or meant only for huge mega-churches, or they are so complex that only the most gifted of leaders seem to be able to "pull it off" and actually grow a church.

It wasn't supposed to be this way!

Jesus gave us a simple template to follow, which would define a compelling and enduring vision for any church. It is found in Acts 1:8:

> "[...] but you will receive power when the Holy Spirit has come upon you; and you shall be My witnesses both in Jerusalem, and in all Judea and Samaria, and even to the uttermost part of the earth." (NASB)

Statistics tell us that about 2/3 of churches across America are at a plateau or in decline. This book is meant to help stop that.

This book will help any pastor or church leader use Acts 1:8 as a template to define a compelling vision for your church. I first learned this in 2007, after 28 years of challenging ministry. Only recently have I felt like I finally know how to lead according to vision.

Ask anyone from our church who has been here since we launched this vision in 2008 and they will agree—this template that we call "The God-Sized Vision" (GSV) has transformed our church. You'll read about that process and about other churches that have followed and incorporated a God-Sized Vision into their own churches leading to incredible fruits. I believe that you, too, can experience the same for your church. After all, Jesus told it to us, because that is what He wanted for us!

The Acts 1:8 "God-Sized Vision" is for Churches of Any Size

Jesse Rubio is the pastor of "Fuentes De Agua Viva," a Hispanic congregation in the near east side of Dayton, Ohio. Our churches have been partners together for the past several years. About two years ago he began to adopt the principles in this book, and prayerfully developed a "God-Sized Vision" for their congregation of about fifty people.

It has been exciting to hear him give updates to how his "GSV" is transforming their congregation. They have a clear understanding of what their focus is, whether it is in their "Jerusalem, Judea, Samaria, or Uttermost Parts of the Earth."

They have relocated to a great building and have more than doubled in size. People are stepping into leadership roles. Discipleship and children's ministries are growing, and they just raised their first $1,200 to invest in Africa (their "Uttermost part" of the world).

Pastor Kevin Ward planted "Potter's Wheel Church" eight years ago in Mbabane, Swaziland. In this city of approximately 80,000 people, Potter's Wheel has grown from a few dozen people to a weekly attendance of about 600. Over 1,200 people consider it to be their church home. The congregation is a wonderful mosaic; proven by the sight of wealthy executives from international companies gladly worshiping alongside native Swazi's who walked to church.

Appendix four shows a picture of Pastor Kevin, as he "vision casted" their version of the "God-Sized Vision" Their church hosts several ministries, from residential Christ-centered rehab programs for men and women, to orphan-care outreaches and life skills training schools. Each of these is part of a well **discerned**, **defined**, and **declared** God-Sized Vision that is getting **done**!

I have been the lead pastor at Christian Life Center (CLC) in Dayton, Ohio since 1990. CLC has over 3,000 people who consider it their church home, with an average of around 2,300 attending on a weekend. This book is about how the "God-Sized Vision" began by transforming us. With an open heart and mind, I pray you will read this book and consider the possibilities for your church, regardless of size.

This Book is One of Three That Work Well Together

This book is one of three practical tools written by this author (available on Amazon.com and Createspace) that go together to contribute to church health in a straightforward, effective way. It is highly recommended to read all three and apply the principles together. Those who have done so have experienced encouraging results:

1. *Teach Them to Give*
2. *The Financially Healthy Church*
3. *BIG: A God-Sized Vision for Your Church* (Using Acts 1:8 as a template for your church health and growth)

After reading *BIG,* you'll find *The Financially Healthy Church* and *Teach Them to Give* will be helpful. Leading a church well means also being a good steward of not only the vision, but also the resources necessary to fuel the work of the church.

Chapter One: How to Use This Book

This book is meant to help churches **Discern, Define, Declare** and **Do** a "God-Sized Vision" for their situation, according to the straightforward template Jesus left us in His words, as recorded in Acts 1:8.

You'll notice a bit of overkill throughout this book. Every time you see **Discern, Define, Declare** and **Do,** it will be in **bold** letters. It cannot be emphasized enough that these are the essential steps needed to propel your church forward into the unique vision God has for you.

Most churches do some of these steps. Few churches do all four consistently. I have come to learn that all four steps, done consistently, are key to the kind of progress God intends for the church to experience. So, just as scripture often uses repetition to make a point, I'll do the same here. Hopefully, after reading and applying this book to your church setting, **Discern, Define, Declare** and **Do** will be second nature to how you do ministry.

Each chapter will be accompanied with discussion and application questions. I would encourage readers to prayerfully consider them, jot down some responses, and then find forums for meaningful dialogue about them. (Perhaps in board or staff meetings, leadership meetings, etc.). This isn't intended to just be a book that you read, rather, it is intended to be a book you also do; first with your leaders, and then live it out with your church.

The appendix includes various subjects of interest for additional reading. The material isn't included in the immediate text, so as not to distract readers from the primary focus of this book.

Keep in mind that doing this book will already set you apart from so many churches destined to stay stuck. You are willing to exercise the discipline and courage to consider challenging questions. You are willing to honestly search for more. No longer is status quo, and hoping for results good enough.

Once you use this book to help you get started and you begin to **Discern**, **Define**, **Declare** and **Do** a God-Sized-Vision of your own, you'll find it helpful to re-visit this book and do the process again as time goes on. After writing this book, and as a last step before publishing it, I decided to try it out on the leadership team at CLC once more.

We completed an all-day session with our leadership staff and church board, about thirty individuals in all. As suggested, we each read and completed the book ahead of time. Then, we spent the day in small groups, talking through each chapter. At the end of each chapter discussion I facilitated a large group discussion.

By the end of the day, we had prayed about and discussed thoughts and conclusions about the next steps to help us define our "God-Sized Vision for the next three years. I wrote our conclusions down on giant marker pads, and we now have the beginning input for clarifying the next phase of our "God-Sized Vision" for our church.

We gained a helpful insight from our day together. The process of **Discern**, **Define**, **Declare** and **Do** is really a circular one. Your church will (or should be) in an ongoing process of pursuing and renewing the vision for your congregation.

For us at Christian Life Center, we have just completed over five and a half years of our "GSV." It has been a terrific season of purposeful ministry and growth for our church. You'll read about it throughout the chapters of this book.

Now that many goals have been achieved, it is time for us to pursue the process all over again to gain greater clarity about our next phase. The following drawing helps illustrate this:

The God-Sized-Vision Process:

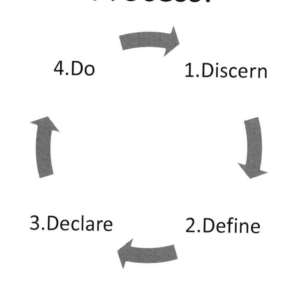

4.Do

1.Discern

3.Declare

2.Define

Chapter Two: A Compelling Vision

The solutions in this book became clear to me while our church was at an in-between stage and I was struggling for clarity. I had been the lead pastor of the same church for 18 years. We had many ministry "successes," and we had the reputation of being a successful, growing church. *But something was missing.*

While I thought I knew all about mission and vision statements, core values, and strategic ministry plans, I realize now that I had a lot to learn. In the past five years, I have learned more about what a compelling vision is and how to declare it than in all the previous years serving the same church combined.

We had a mission statement that everyone seemed to accept, but it wasn't enough. Many other churches could acknowledge this as well. There are countless church mission statements, but after the motivating feeling of saying or hearing the statement, things fall flat. There isn't a lot of life or momentum driven by the mission statement. In far too many situations, as you get to know and experience the church, you get the feeling that the mission statement is more like wishful thinking rather than a true statement of reality or future intention.

Many churches have a mission statement comprised of catchy, inspiring sayings to explain why their church exists. However, knowing why you exist can still leave uncertainty regarding what direction to pursue. A mission statement answers the question of "Why?" it doesn't answer the question "What are we supposed to do?" Mission statements typically stay the same over time.

This is not to disparage mission statements, or the need for pastors to cast an effective vision. Indeed, for a church to grow there must be a clear and compelling vision for the pastor, leaders and congregation to follow. Without it, the church (or any organization) will falter.

That's where a vision statement comes in and makes a difference. A vision statement is different. A vision statement answers the question, "What does it look like, at any given point in time, when and as you accomplish the mission?"

Proverbs 29:18 tells us "Without a vision people are 'unrestrained.' The King James Version states that such vision-less people "perish." The Bible makes it clear to us what today's leaders affirm: whether in a church or a corporation, vision is essential for any group of people to maximize their potential.

The idea of people being "unrestrained" is like a thoroughbred race horse left in the pasture alone with no saddle on its back, no bridle on its head, and no bit in its mouth, no rider, and no reigns. This may conjure up images of a peaceful grazing animal, but it is not the way the horse wins. For all that horsepower to run at full capacity and cross the finish line, the necessary restraints must be applied.

> Likewise, churches aren't meant to "graze" aimlessly in the field of church work.

Likewise, churches aren't meant to graze aimlessly in the field of church work. However, left to their own meanderings, most churches will seldom realize their potential without the restraint that vision provides. Answers to the questions of "What are we trying to do? Why are we trying to do it? How will we accomplish it? What resources do we need to acquire or save?" are all restraints that need clear direction. Once given and ascribed to, such restraints can help limit distractions while propelling people forward to great gains.

The problem is that far too many pastors do not know how to **Discern**, **Define**, **Declare** and **Do** a clear and compelling vision. Lay leaders in their congregations are often left feeling frustrated or at a loss for what to do. *These loyal lay leaders may be guided by vision in the workplace, but they often aren't sure what vision should look like in the church.*

Unfortunately, this is not an isolated problem. In a study by The Barna Group, only 4% of pastors identify leadership as their primary gift.[1] Most pastors have relational pastoral gifts. They love providing care for their flock, they are often great students of the Bible, and are gifted teachers. However, leading their congregation to grow and achieve is something many pastors struggle with. *This*

---

[1]The Barna Group. (2002, January 7). Pastors rate themselves highly, especially as teachers. Retrieved from: www.barna.org/barna-update/65pastors-rate-themselves-highly.

book is intended for pastors who struggle with the whole "vision thing." It is intended to help you follow some basic Biblical steps to **Discern**, **Define**, **Declare** and **Do** a compelling vision that can begin to move your congregation forward in fruitful vision-focused efforts.

This is also for pastors, who may indeed be gifted leaders, but your leadership (and the momentum of your congregation) seems to ebb and flow with passing interests, projects, and ideas. You need a long-term sense of direction that can stabilize you and your congregation for ongoing effectiveness. No more "flash in the pan" excitement. You want a vision that will last.

Finally, this book is for lay people who want to come alongside a pastor, to help serve the church by helping to clarify and pursue its vision for the future. Perhaps you have leadership abilities of your own. Perhaps you have financial or other resources you are eager to invest in a church that seems to be truly making a difference. You want your expenditure of time and finances to matter, and are eager, but unsure of how to help your pastor get there from here.

The wonderful thing is that this vision statement is Biblically based and can be translated to any church. If adhered to, a God-Sized Vision will propel you and your congregation forward to an exciting future. Because this vision is Biblically based on the words of Jesus, it transcends culture. I have seen this same vision applied in a Hispanic urban congregation in the United States, as well as in a thriving congregation in Swaziland, Africa. I am amazed at what it has done for and through each of our churches. I trust that you will be too.

Chapter Three: A Mid-Night Answer to "Now What?"

I remember going to bed after a forum hosted by a mission organization our church supports, Book of Hope. They do an amazing job distributing the Bible around the world, in a host of different languages (www.bookofhope.com).

Our church was in one of those waiting phases having a sense of direction, doing a lot of things right, but waiting for clarity of what the next season would look like for us. We had a great mission statement, *"To Know God, Be His People, Value Others, and Change Our World."* We've had the same mission statement for two decades, and I don't see it changing soon. It clearly states why our church exists.

However, we were at an impasse. We needed to answer the question, "Where were we to focus our resources to pursue the mission for our church for the next several years, and what would it look like when we achieved it?"

I woke up at about 3:00 a.m. After restlessly trying to fall back to sleep, I realized it was one of those 'Psalm 4:4 moments.' I was meant to "Meditate in [my] heart on [my] bed and be still." I did just that, and spent the next four hours in meditation and prayer. I remember asking God, "Now what? What are we supposed to be focusing on for the next several years, and what does it look like?"

For those four hours, my mind was crystal clear, and it seemed like all we had been doing as a church fell into place, along

> In launching the "God-Sized Vision," we simply wanted to discover and follow God's next steps for us. We wanted to do it according to Biblical principles. And we wanted to do it in a way that we could inspect and celebrate the fruit of our investments.

with new insights of where we needed to go in the future. I could even imagine how I would draw a picture to explain this new direction. When my wife woke up at 7:00 a.m., I told her, "I think I just got clarity on where our church is supposed to go for the next 5 to 7 years."

Since we had a plane to catch, I waited until we were in the air to tell her about the results of my four hour prayer time. I eagerly put down my tray table, turned a boarding pass over, and drew for her what has become known around our church as "The God-Sized Vision." Little did I know that in addition to being on a plane headed for home, I was drawing clarification for our church's future and put us on a journey that would take us forward like no other time in our history.

A brief recap of some of the progress in the first five years of following the "God-Sized Vision" will affirm the fruitfulness of our journey.

First, we built a 28,000 square foot addition to our main campus to facilitate discipleship and relational growth, *and paid cash for it* without having to raise the funds (approximately $3 million).

Second, we have added two satellite campuses that are each attended by 100 to 200 people. We are now "One Church in Four Locations."

Third, we have budgeted up to $120,000 a year to invest in 10 inner city partner churches, to grow their spiritual imprint in our urban neighborhoods.

Fourth, we have built three holistic church campuses in Swaziland, Africa at a cost of about $150,000 each. We have also packaged and sent over 1.2 million fortified rice meals to this tiny nation where 75% of the people live on less than one dollar a day. In all, we have invested over $1.5 million in these African church planting efforts.

In Addition, we have invested about $200,000 into our medical partners in Swaziland, The Luke Commission (See Appendix). This includes helping with phase one of building a "miracle campus" that will not only be the base of medical outreach in Swaziland, but to other countries across Africa as well.

Beyond all these advances, during this same period our church invested approximately $3.2 million in our foreign missions and outreach programs, and we also experienced congregational growth of about 20% over the half-decade.

Admittedly, these aren't the kind of outcomes that typically get noticed at national seminars or publicized in popular book deals. However, that wasn't our goal. In launching the "God-Sized Vision," we simply wanted to discover and follow God's next steps *for us.* We wanted to do it according to Biblical principles. And we wanted to do it in a way we could inspect and celebrate the fruit of our investment of time, finances, and attention.

As I have shared the "God-Sized Vision" with other churches, it appears to provide a template for a compelling Biblical vision that other churches can effectively pursue, regardless of congregational size. The simplicity of it is also encouraging for pastors who struggle with the whole "vision thing" and for lay people who aren't sure how strategic principles apply to church work.

Questions for Consideration:

1. The Bible makes it clear that God expects and inspects fruit from our life together as "the church." It is important for us to celebrate these fruits of our ministry efforts for Christ's sake. (Read John 15:1-8)

   A. Make a list of three or four fruitful results of your church's recent efforts.

   _____

   _____

   _____

   _____

   _____

   _____

   B. What positive impact did these outcomes have on your church? (Emotional, motivational, relational, spiritual, financial, etc.)_____

   _____

   _____

   _____

   _____

   _____

2. Churches often try to function without a clear plan or strategy for ministry. Why do you suppose this is?

   _____

   _____

   _____

   _____

   _____

   _____

Chapter Four: It Truly is "One Size Fits All"

It seems most of the churches we read about in contemporary leadership are several thousands of people, way beyond the average church of about 100 people in attendance each weekend. As such, it's often hard to translate their approach to ministry to a smaller setting. The pattern suggested here, in light of Acts 1:8 is clear, and translatable to any size church.

Our church currently averages in the 2,300 to 2,700 range for weekend attendance, including adults and children at all campuses. We've had our ups and downs in this five year period, but the consistent positive trajectory we are on has been from following the "God-Sized Vision."

While we are considered a "mega-church" (more than 2,000 in attendance), these numbers aren't outstanding in terms of the national spotlight. That's Okay...most of us aren't national standouts anyway. *Lest the leader from a small congregation immediately dismiss this as "big-church ideas," I would suggest that it is Jesus' idea, and has proven to be appropriate for churches of any size.*

Consider Pastor Jesse. Pastor Jesse is the senior pastor of Fountains of Living Waters church ("Fuentes de Agua Viva" in Spanish). His is one of our partner churches and we have invested both man-hours and finances in what was a fledgling congregation. He too has adopted the "God-sized Vision" (GSV) approach to ministry, and he recently told our partner pastors that it is transforming his congregation. They have recently relocated to an awesome church facility, they are growing in number,

> ...she came up to me after service, and with believable enthusiasm, said to me what I suspect the average pastor longs to hear, "Pastor Stan, I just LOVE tithing to this church!"

they have increased their discipleship for children and adults, and they are expanding their world outreach (missions) ministry.

Just as the five purposes of a church from Rick Warren's *Purpose Driven Church* can apply to every congregation (listed in the appendix), I believe the GSV is appropriate and applicable for any and every church.[2] Furthermore, it is simple and clear to understand. Your GSV can (and should) start out small and grow over time. In addition, it has proven to be energizing to many congregations.

A perfect example of how motivating the GSV is can be found in a brief conversation I had with "Michal," a middle aged woman who had been attending our church for several months. One Sunday, after casting the current phase of the "God-Sized Vision," she came up to me after service with believable enthusiasm and said to me what I suspect the average pastor longs to hear, "Pastor Stan, I just LOVE tithing to this church!"

You may be wondering "What a "God-Sized Vision" is, and what it entails. It is a divinely insightful direction that Jesus gave to his followers just before He left this planet. It is a clear verse of instruction that can literally become a simple template for a church to answer the question, "What do we do now?"

The answer is found in Acts 1:8. Jesus gave the disciples enduring direction for the church:

> "But you will receive power when the Holy Spirit has come upon you, and you will be my witnesses in Jerusalem, and in all Judea and Samaria, and to the uttermost parts of the earth." (NASB)

> While many churches, pastors and lay members languish without a clear vision, Acts 1:8 provides a simple four dimensional guide for leading churches forward to an exciting future.

---

[2] Rick Warren. (1995). *The Purpose Driven Church*. Grand Rapids, MI: Zondervan.

This simple verse answers the question for churches and church leaders everywhere: "What are we supposed to do? What is our vision for future action?" *Surprisingly, like a buried treasure, this truth has been before us all along, waiting to be rediscovered.* While many congregations, pastors, and lay members languish without a clear vision, Acts1:8 provides a simple four dimensional guide to leading churches forward to an exciting future.

Questions for consideration:

1. What is your church's mission statement and how well are people in your church acquainted with it? From memory, write it here:

_____

_____

_____

_____

For a good "reality check" you might conduct an informal poll, asking people to fill out a simple 4 item questionnaire:
   A.   What is our mission statement?
   B.   What do you personally do to help your church achieve it?
   C.   What goals are we as a church pursuing because of it?
   D.   What "fruit" can we objectively point to as a result of it?

The important thing to look for in responses is consistency. Do people seem to be on the same page? Does the mission apply to them personally, and does it clearly direct the focus of the church? Is it making a God-Sized difference?

_____

_____

_____

2. **Discern, Define, Declare** and **Do** are the four essential responsibilities related to vision for leaders in regard to imparting the vision to those they lead. On a scale of 1 to 10, how well do you feel you are currently doing in each of these four essential areas? Rate these based on how you think the church leadership is doing as a whole, in each area.

    (Note: it is best if you answer these *after* you have conducted the informal poll above. This will guard against unfounded, unrealistic optimism that doesn't give you a clear picture of how you are truly doing. Most church leaders over-rate effectiveness in these areas without some objective feedback like this.)

A. **Discern**: Key leaders in the church praying and sharing together in order to sense what priorities God is laying on your heart as a church.

1 to 10: _____ (Where 1 is not at all, and 10 is always)

Comment:

_____

_____

B. **Define**: Intentionally taking the time to clarify what the vision components are, what the outcomes should be, and what resources are required (time, people, and finances) and the steps to get there.

1 to 10: _____

Comment:

_____

_____

C. **Declare**: How effectively, consistently, and comprehensively is the vision communicated to the congregation? This is evidenced by widespread awareness of what the vision is, as well as comprehensive "buy in," and pervasive participation in accomplishing it.

1 to 10: _____

Comment:

_____

_____

D. **Do**: To what degree do we put our time, energy and money where our mouth is? (So-to-speak). Note: This is a crucial question. If you can't show an abundance of tangible evidences of how the vision affects your decisions and behavior in reality, you aren't there yet.

1 to 10: _____

Comment:

_____

_____

The above questions will be most beneficial if your leadership team(s) discuss them as a group *after* answering them privately. You'll find it interesting to hear how others perceive current vision effectiveness, as well as perceptions of the congregation as a whole.

Don't be surprised if you see significant variation in responses. That is ok for now as a certain lack of cohesiveness is pretty common. Reading and working through this book is intended to help get your leaders and your church on the same page.

Chapter Five: The "God-Sized Vision" Template

I'm a pretty visual communicator, so drawings help me grasp concepts (Our staff claims that a meeting with drawing is a good meeting!). Below is a simple chart-like representation of the GSV. Across the top is a "God-Sized" kind of claim (imagine inserting the name of your church at __)

Building the Church, Changing our World, a God-Sized Vision for_____Acts 1:8

(Our) Jerusalem	Judea	Samaria	Uttermost Parts

Beneath this heading is a reference to Acts 1:8, and four columns that represent the four dimensions of this vision: Jerusalem, Judea, Samaria, and the "Uttermost Parts of the World."

A brief explanation of each column (dimension) is helpful:

Most of us are not aware of ancient Middle Eastern geography, but a quick look at a map indicates that Jesus was calling His followers to spread the Gospel outward, in geographically concentric circles, until the whole world would be reached.

First, they were to begin right where they were (*Jerusalem*). Jesus wanted His followers to reach out to their family, friends, coworkers and the community in which they lived. They were to be "salt and light" and share a message of transformation through the love of God.

Next, the "Good News" was expected to spread across the neighboring geographic region (*Judea*). The early disciples weren't just to launch the church in Jerusalem, but to also populate the surrounding regions with the message of Jesus Christ.

Third, by calling for the spread of the Gospel into Samaria, Jesus was letting His followers know this wasn't just for Jews. Taking the "Good News" to Samaria indicates that the Gospel should be taken into cross-cultural settings (the Samaritans were similar, yet markedly different from the Jews, with culturally charged tensions between them).

> The one constant was people everywhere needed the Good News of Jesus Christ. That was true then, and it is still true today.

Finally, the Gospel was to travel internationally to the rest of the world ("Uttermost parts"). For New Testament disciples, that meant taking Christianity to lands and people far different than those in the Jerusalem church. Customs, cultures and languages were different. The one constant was people everywhere needed the Good News of Jesus Christ. That was true then, and it is still true today.

A later chapter will explain how this four dimensional vision from Acts 1:8 so simply translates to churches today. *Understanding Acts 1:8 as providing a fourfold template for ministry has helped us, it has helped others who have adopted this vision, and it can help your church as well. Below is a completed version of what the "God-Sized Vision" template looks like for our church.*

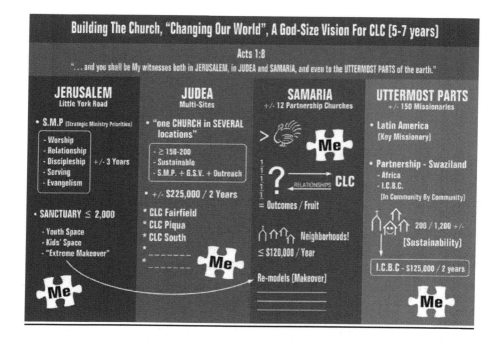

Questions for consideration:

1. The first part of Acts 1:8 makes it clear that the spread of the Gospel is dependent upon the empowering work of the Holy Spirit in the lives of believers. Identify three gifts of the Spirit listed in scripture, and explain briefly how they are helpful in this work (Romans 12: 4-8; 1 Corinthians 12:7-12; Ephesians 4: 11, 12).

   _____

   _____

   _____

   _____

   _____

   _____

2. Galatians 5:22, 23 lists the Christ-like character qualities called the "Fruit of the Spirit." Read the passage, then select two and identify how the Fruit of the Spirit helps add validity to the works we do to spread the Gospel.

   _____

   _____

   _____

   _____

   _____

   _____

Chapter Six: Failure to Launch

My wife's first response to my 'back-of-the-boarding-pass' drawing was "Where do you want me to be involved in that?" This was a great and encouraging question. I wish the first response from our church board would have been as receptive.

It was only about two weeks after our trip to Book of Hope, I was excited to be in our monthly church board meeting. On the white board in my office, I drew with great enthusiasm the "God-Sized Vision" that was the outcome of my mid-night prayer time. I showed how the vision was Biblically based on the final words of Jesus, how it was comprehensive in its scope, covering every aspect of the church, and a perfect fit for where we were and where we needed to go over the next five to seven years. On top of it all, it was totally consistent with our mission *"To Know God, Be His People, Value Others, and Change Our World."*

Once I stopped talking and set my marker pen down, I remember asking something like "Well, what do you think?" In hindsight, the moment was not unlike the times I would stop by the National Trapshooting Championships held only a few miles from our home. Hundreds of competitors, armed with shotguns, yell out to an operator crouched in a cement box about 50 feet ahead of them to "Pull" as the target goes sailing, and bam! They shoot it to pieces.

> I also learned something else that is a little harder for my action-oriented personality to accept; vision takes time.

The board grew silent and shifted in their seats. Then, one member simply said "That's a lot of work." The tone wasn't optimistic in nature. A second member folded their arms across his chest and said "You don't have the people here to accomplish that." At that moment I could have sworn I heard someone say "Pull!"

A couple more supportive and open minded members spoke up favorably, but the tone had been set and it wasn't encouraging. Thankfully, we concluded the meeting in agreement that we would pray about it. We also decided that we would appoint a task team to prayerfully "drill into" the ideas and come up with thoughts and recommendations on whether or not this was a viable direction for our church.

A month or so later, after the board was open to the concept, I shared the "God Sized-Vision" with our leadership staff to get their perspective on it as well. For the next six months, I re-drew the "God-Sized Vision" many times on that marker board, on note pads, and in my mind. We discussed it, prayed about it, researched it, wrestled with it, argued about it, let it sit, and came back to it.

In the process, I learned a few things. First, I have realized the truly essential nature of vision. Without it, Proverbs makes it clear, people "perish." I also learned something else that is a little harder for my action-oriented personality to accept: vision takes time. A vision that gets launched prematurely is hard to follow, and even harder to sustain, especially as that vision involves increasing amounts of people, resources, and time.

> A vision that gets launched prematurely is hard to follow, and even harder to sustain, especially as that vision involves an increasing amount of people, finances, and time.

In retrospect, I'm glad for the initial hesitation on that February evening when I first drew the "God-Sized Vision" for our board. The reluctance forced me, and us, to wrestle with the details and implications of the vision so when it was finally ready to be "**declared**" publicly, it was what it needed to be.

By the end of August, six long months later, we were clear and united; agreeing to what we had **discerned** would be the next leg of our journey. *We agreed that the vision was indeed going to be a lot of work. It was going to be expensive. We understood the vision would require spiritual effort through a united church to pursue it and faith to believe God would do this through us. We also agreed that for our church, it was right.*

Questions for consideration:

1. **Discern**, **Define**, **Declare** and **Do** has been the suggested order of pursuing the "God-Sized Vision" for your church. Identify and discuss a time when you were part of or saw an effort in a church (or other organization) that switched up this order. (Perhaps "Do" was first, or "Discern or Define" never really happened, or something got "Declared" before truly being "Defined," etc.)_____

   _____

   _____

   _____

   _____

   _____

2. Matthew 28:19, 20 is another way to state the mission Jesus declared in Acts 1:8. It is commonly called "The Great Co-Mission" for Christ and His church, empowered by the Holy Spirit. (Hyphen added for emphasis). Read these verses. How does this passage make it clear that Jesus expects our "witness" referred to in Acts 1:8 to be practical and life-transforming, (more than just declaring the Gospel truth)?

   _____

   _____

   _____

   _____

   _____

   _____

3. What does "empowered by the Holy Spirit" look like in your life, your family, and your church?

   _____

   _____

   _____

   _____

   _____

Chapter Seven: Ready, Set, GO!

September 6 and 7 of 2008 is one of those weekends that people in our church call a milestone. Without any exaggeration whatsoever, anyone who has been around CLC for any length of time before that will tell you the vision drawn and declared that day has changed us forever. I'm so grateful for that.

I remember that Saturday afternoon when I was in my office following my typical weekend routine. I always practice preaching my message in my office out loud before I do so in a sanctuary full of people.

I drew the "God-Sized Vision" on my marker board just as I would four more times for each of the live services at our home campus that weekend. After I completed the drawing, I stood back and looked it over when a small "voice" simply said, *"That sure is going to be a lot of work."* I was sobered by the thought, took a deep breath, and silently agreed.

Then, another thought came to me and sounded something like: *"You wouldn't really have to do this. The church is big enough and no one will think any less of us continuing on as we are. Everyone seems satisfied. Why go to all the bother and the risk?"* For a moment, I wondered if this new sense of vision was just a function of my sometimes too-driven personality. Couldn't I be happy with a large church that is doing many good things? After all, no-one was forcing me to do this, certainly not the church board. If anything, I had spent the past six months trying to get everyone, including the board, *on* board with this vision.

> For a moment, I wondered if this new sense of vision was just a function of my sometimes too-driven personality. Couldn't I be happy with a large church that is doing many good things? After all, no-one was "pushing" me to do this...

Thankfully, five years later, as I look back I'm grateful that I didn't listen to my apprehensions. Instead, I preached the same sermon four times that weekend. Each service, with a fresh four foot by eight foot sheet of "foam core" board for my drawing surface, *I took several colored markers, and drew us into the future of our church.*

We ended up saving a few of those original boards. In fact, we used one of them recently at a series of "dessert socials" in September of 2013, five years after it was first drawn into existence. We celebrated all that God has done through that vision over the past five years, and looked ahead at what the continued future of the "God-Sized-Vision" based on Acts 1:8 would mean for us. Believe it or not, the future is even more daunting than what it seemed to be the first weekend I drew on those marker boards. However, now with five years of "God-Sized" experience, this daunting vision is compellingly inviting!

> I took several colored markers, and drew us into the future of our church.

We learned in 2008 that after **Discerning** and **Defining** the vision, **Declaring** the vision for the first time is just the first public step, of many. Thankfully, the weekend seemed to go well and the vision was met with warm acceptance. Truth be known, looking back I believe people accepted the vision sermon largely based on people being kind to me as their pastor , as much or more than their belief that this was a new era for us.

The next step to launching this "God-Sized-Vision" was as important as preaching the vision. We needed to *pray* the vision as a congregation. We produced a DVD to be played at each of our small groups, as a sort of "plug-and-play" prayer time. We asked all of our small groups to host a prayer meeting by using the DVD. In doing this, we were able to get about half of our adults involved in the most important spiritual work of launching the vision—prayer.

The DVD was divided into four parts. I would talk for about 10 minutes, summarizing each of the four dimensions (Jerusalem, Judea, Samaria, and the Uttermost Parts). I would also give suggested prayer directions for each area, then, the group leader would pause the DVD and small group prayer time would begin.

This was an essential step in launching our new vision. From the very beginning of our journey, this began what has become an ongoing priority for us: prayer for our vision. Since that time, we dedicate the first Wednesday evening of each month as a worship and prayer service. We regularly pray for some dimension of our GSV during these meetings. I am convinced much of our progress made in pursuit of our vision has been due to the progress we first make in prayer during these monthly gatherings.

Following is a picture of the original "God-Sized Vision" board drawing (it will make more sense as you read further).

The next step to launching this "God-Sized Vision" was as important as preaching the vision. We needed to *pray* the vision as a congregation.

The "God-Sized Vision" Board, drawn for Christian Life
Center, September 2008:

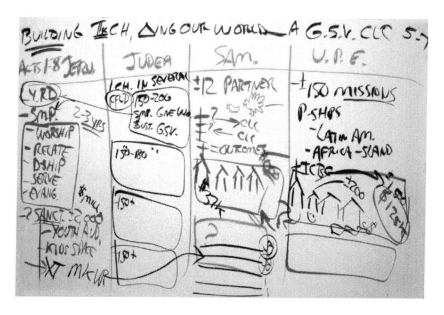

Questions for consideration:

1. The outpouring of the Holy Spirit that would later launch the Acts 1:8 vision was birthed at a prayer meeting of 120 people. Acts 1:14 specifically mentions that they were united. Why is it important for a church to be united in order to pursue a "God-Sized Vision?"

    _____
    _____
    _____
    _____
    _____
    _____

2. Unfortunately, it is possible to launch out in a well-intended ministry effort without much prayer. What does praying help accomplish that makes it so important to ministry fruitfulness?

    _____
    _____
    _____
    _____
    _____
    _____

3. Why is it important to continue to pray about a "God-Sized Vision" once a church **Discerns**, **Defines**, **Declares**, and starts to **Do** one?

    _____
    _____
    _____
    _____
    _____
    _____

Chapter Eight: Defining Our "Jerusalem"

Over the past five years, we have found the "four columns" described in Acts 1:8 represent four dimensions of the ministry of the local church. They are timeless, straightforward, and easily understood. If every church were committed to them, the world-changing impact of today's church would be staggering.

For the next four chapters, I'm going to pose a question to help you define the God-Sized Vision for your church.

For your Jerusalem, which is your home campus, ask the question:

What priorities should we pursue to make our church location as spiritually and relationally healthy as possible?

Jerusalem: For us, Jerusalem relates to all things pertaining to our "Little York Road Campus." This 33 acre tract of land is the original site for our church as "Christian Life Center" since the congregation relocated there, on interstate 70, in 1981.

Around the time of launching the God-Sized Vision I heard Gary Haugen of the International Justice Mission (www.ijm.org) speak at the Willow Creek Leadership Summit.[3] I still haven't forgotten his convicting critique of the American church. While I'm sure I have not recalled his message verbatim, I have not forgotten his challenge. He stated that there are more resources today for Christians than ever before in the history of Christianity. There are CD's, Podcasts, DVD's, conferences, music, the best teachers at the click of a mouse or remote control; yet, our society is more in need of Christ than perhaps any other time in our history. In addition, those who study the American church tell us there is little statistical difference in the lifestyles and world views of Christians compared to Non-Christians. (Barna....)[4]

"Why?" Haugen asked, "Do you suppose this is so? What is wrong, that the most resourced church in the history of Christianity is failing to transform its culture?"

---

[3] Gary Haugen. "Just Courage: Charging the Darkness." The Leadership Summit. August, 2008.

[4] The Barna Group. (2004, May 24). Faith has a Limited Effect on Most People's Behavior. Retrieved from: https://www.barna.org/barna-update/article/5-barna-update/188-faith-has-a-limited-effect-on-most-peoples-behavior.

He proposed an explanation I have tried to repeat many times. Haugen went on to suggest that many American Christians can be compared to body builders in health clubs. In health clubs, Haugen suggests that body builders often build massive muscle for the wrong reason. Too often, body builders build big muscles simply so they can pose! (Haugen mimicked a body builder posing in front of a mirror). He went on to claim, "Muscles aren't made for POSING...they are made for doing work!"

He then makes the obvious and challenging comparison by asking the question, "Have we, the church, forgotten that all the blessings and power from God are for us to go out and do the WORK of the church in the world?" Many of today's Christians consume the blessings and presence of God in order to "pose" rather than to do God's work; we tend to develop and "flex" spiritual muscles, as body builders do. We have extravagant services, sing worship songs, hold Bible studies, all as an end in themselves, not as a way to say, "Great, now let's go out and change our world

We at Christian Life Center (CLC) want to be a healthy (muscular) church for the purpose of going out to actually do the work and the ministry that God has called us to do. For us, that means making a difference where we live (Jerusalem) and then going into our version of "Judea" and "Samaria" and even to the "Uttermost Parts of the World."

For our Jerusalem focus, we identify Rick Warren's "Five Purposes of a Church" as priorities for our ministry attention. As such,

> We believe a growing and healthy "Jerusalem" is essential to a growing and healthy "God-Sized Vision." This statement is critically important to us. We don't want to grow simply for the sake of being a big church. We want to grow, to sustain a growing "God-Sized Vision" from our church.

we try to prioritize becoming a healthy church in these areas:

1. **Relationships**: do what we can to make our church a place where you can know and be known (no strangers or lone rangers).
2. **Discipleship**: intentionally growing together in our understanding of what it means to follow Christ. And then, doing so accordingly.
3. **Serving:** using our gifts and talents to serve others in our church family.
4. **Evangelism:** reaching those close to us, as well as those around the world.
5. **Worship:** corporately and individually celebrating the presence of God.[5]

The Purpose Driven Church can help any congregation trying to define their priorities to understand the importance of each of these areas in the church. In addition to this resource, we currently alternate annually between taking the Natural Church Development Assessment (Church Smart Resources),[6] and The REVEAL Survey (Willow Creek Association).[7] We find that by taking an objective evaluation of our church health every year, we have a clearer picture of how we are doing at our Little York Campus (our Jerusalem). We find that this objective assessment of our body's health is important to keep us focused on the right internal (Jerusalem focused) priorities.

We believe a growing and healthy "Jerusalem" is essential to a growing and healthy "God-Sized Vision." This statement is critically important to us. We don't want to grow for the sake of being a big church. We want growth that is both stimulated by and sustaining of our God-Sized Vision.

---

[5] Rick Warren. (2005). *The Purpose Driven Church*. Grand Rapids, MI: Zondervan.
[6] National Church Development (NCD). (2014, August). Retrieved from: www.ncd-international.org/public/index.html.
[7] The Willow Creek Association. (2014). *Reveal* Retrieved from: http://engagechurches.com/reveal.

Questions for consideration:

1. Using the definitions above, evaluate how well your church is doing in each of the five key purposes of a church. Put a "plus" sign (+) next to those you feel are your greatest strengths. Put an "equal" sign (=) next to those that don't necessarily help or hinder your church. Put a "minus" sign (-) next to those that definitely need to improve:

   A. Relationships _____
   B. Discipleship _____
   C. Serving _____
   D. Evangelism _____ (Think primarily about reaching people somehow connected to those who attend your Jerusalem: relatives, friends, co-workers, neighbors, classmates, etc.)
   E. Worship _____

2. Regarding your answers in the previous question, jot down three possible **simple** action steps to improve areas you rated as either = or - (Such opportunities are often referred to as "Low hanging fruit.")

   _____
   _____
   _____
   _____
   _____

Chapter Nine: Defining Our "Judea"

As the Gospel spread across Judea, the church grew. While not identical to Jerusalem, reaching Judea was still reaching similar people, in a similar culture. The church spread in the early chapters of the Book of Acts, among like people, across the surrounding region.

The question for the "Judea" dimension of your God-Sized vision is:

What can we do to support the cause of church multiplication across our region?

Before you panic and claim that your congregation just isn't big enough or healthy enough to plant a church, let me explain. We have found it helpful to consider Judea as having to do with church multiplication. For us, we have a "multi-site" strategy of reaching our greater Dayton community (the region has about 500,000 residents spread out across several counties). Our current "God-Sized Vision" goal is to have at least four multi-site congregations throughout our community, in addition to our original campus at Little York Road.

> Don't abandon the "God-Sized Vision" principles of Acts 1:8 just because you lead a small congregation.

We have planned to launch sites as frequently as one every other year. We kept this rhythm the first four years but found it necessary to slow the pace between our third and fourth. Launching isn't exactly a "cookie cutter" process and we want to make sure each site is running well before moving on to another. Flexibility and tenacity are key ingredients in pursuing a "God-Sized Vision."

Some churches prefer to plant churches rather than embark on a multi-site strategy. This is just as good! We have tried planting churches in our past and only one of three was very successful, so for us, the multi-site strategy seems to fit our "DNA" best. If God lays it on your heart to plant a church, there are many resources to guide you in this crucial "Kingdom-expanding, Judea-reaching" strategy.

Our advice would be to pray, do your homework, pray some more, reason together, and **discern** and **define** a plan with measurable goals. Then, cast the "Judea piece" of the God-Sized Vision (**Declare**), cast it some more, and then again. When the time is right, get started! (**DO**).

Wait a minute! A brief reality check will identify that the majority of churches in America have somewhere less than 200 people in attendance. It is understandable that many reading this book will quickly dismiss the idea of planting a church, or launching a multi-site congregation because they feel they don't have the size, momentum or resources to do so. I don't blame you.

That's the beauty of the God-Sized Vision approach to your church's vision. Simply and prayerfully ask the question to **discern** "What would suit us?"

Don't abandon the "God-Sized Vision" principles of Acts 1:8 just because you lead a small congregation. The truth still applies. So, what could you do for the cause of church multiplication in your region? Consider Judea as your responsibility to help in planting or multiplying THE church, rather than just focusing on YOUR church.

> With this mindset a whole new world of possibilities opens to you. What can you do, even if only once a year, to help with the cause of multiplying the church?

With this mindset a whole new world of possibilities opens to you. What can you do, even if only once a year, to help with the cause of church multiplication? Perhaps you could find a church plant not far from you and volunteer to canvas their neighborhood in a once-a-year outreach with their congregation. If that seems too big a first step, why not just get your two congregations together, at or near where they meet, for a prayer night with the pastors and members for their church?

If this congregation has a facility, maybe you could do a volunteer work day to help with any maintenance or repairs. Or, if they rent their facility, perhaps you could buy a piece of equipment (a microphone, a new podium, etc.).

Church planters often feel like they are "going it alone." Maybe your "Judea" emphasis would be to invite a planter pastor and their family to a holiday reception at your church. A carry-in dinner along with Christmas presents and then prayer for their family could just be the encouragement they need!

Be creative! Do your homework and your prayerwork. I believe God will speak to you and your church leadership about how your church, at whatever the size, could be a blessing to the cause of church multiplication. The Acts 1:8 concept of the church is that we each share in the responsibility of spreading the body of Christ across our Judea, whether this means across your city, county, state, or the country.

Please, overcome any tendency toward your own needs at this point. For many, it would be easy to say, "We aren't any bigger than some church plants we would be helping!" That isn't the point; the Bible makes it clear it is more blessed to give than to receive. The Acts 1:8 concept is to be outwardly focused. So even if you wish someone was reaching out like this to you, do it anyway! Learn to give from your church to the Acts 1:8 vision. As you do, I assure you, you won't be disappointed.

One last admonition: whatever you do for Judea, do it at least annually. Create an expectation within your congregation of, "What are we going to do this year?" Involve as many people, at as many ages from your church as you can as you do it. You will wonder why you didn't do it sooner. Also, the church plants you help

> Do your homework, and your PRAYERWORK I believe God will speak to you and your church leadership about how your church, at whatever the size, could be a blessing to the cause of church multiplication.

should be culturally similar to yours. Not a different language group, not a huge socioeconomic contrast, and such. As you read further in the "Samaria" aspect of the God-Sized Vision, you'll understand why.

Questions for consideration:

1. Take a moment and consider the New Testament, starting with the book of Acts and throughout most of the Epistles. The spread of the Gospel in the first century after the life of Christ was very much about what we call today "church multiplication." Reflect and then jot down two or three reasons why the establishment of new churches was a key to the spread of the good news of Jesus Christ.

    _____
    _____
    _____
    _____
    _____
    _____

2. "Church multiplication" is perhaps a less limiting term than "church planting." In the past, the idea of planting a church was often left to big churches or denominational offices. Today, churches of any size can contribute to the overall goal of multiplying the number of churches that exist. Brainstorm practical and simple responses below that could contribute to this Biblical priority.

    The exercises below are to get you thinking of baby steps that your church can do in contributing to the cause of church multiplication.

a. What annual holiday activity could your church host for the good of a nearby church plant or for their pastor and/or the pastor's family?

    _____
    _____
    _____

b. What could people from your church do to offer encouragement once a year to a church plant congregation that would be minimal in cost, but high in benefits?

    _____
    _____
    _____

c. List two ideas of outreach activities you could do with a church plant, in their target neighborhood, that would take less than six hours of activity time (planning for it may take more time).

_____

_____

_____

_____

d. Assume a young church has a facility but it needs some "elbow grease." Identify a four hour project that could be done for a church like this, which would cost less than $100.

_____

_____

_____

_____

e. Finally, dream big. List three communities within 100 miles of your church that could use a good church, that someday God might work mightily through your congregation to either launch a satellite or plant a church there (or to partner with other churches as part of a group church multiplication effort). Go ahead and just list the communities by name:

_____

_____

_____

_____

Chapter Ten: Defining Our "Samaria"

One need only read of Jesus' encounter with the Samaritan woman in the fourth chapter of John's gospel to understand that there were strong tensions between the Jews and Samaritans. Considered a compromised ethnic blend of Israelite and Gentile nations, the Samaritans were not only seen as a different people group than the Jews, John 4 indicates tensions between them.

This hostility seems further exacerbated by certain Samaritan religious practices that defied Jewish tradition; not the least of which was insisting on temple worship other than at Jerusalem. Suffice it to say; when Jesus called his followers to take the Gospel to "Samaria", He was calling them to enter into cross-cultural ministry fraught with challenges.

"Cross-cultural" is, by definition, a relative term. To begin to **discern** and **define** what would be cross-cultural for you, you must start by asking, "What culture do we primarily minister in/to?" A series of well thought out questions will help you identify the demographic(s) you most readily reach. For many churches, the congregation is of a primary racial mix. Often, one economic grouping or age demographic is also predominant. Your Samaria focus needs to be culturally different from your own.

> Although we are located on a primary interstate highway at the edge OF our city, we don't believe our address absolves us of a sense of responsibility FOR our city.

The goal of reaching Samaria is not necessarily to bring Samaria to you (recall the extensive 'bus ministries' of a prior era). Jesus was telling His followers to take the Gospel *to* Samaria.

Our question regarding the Samaria piece of your God-Sized Vision is:

What church can we partner with to strengthen their local impact in the Samaria of our area? How do we help this church as they reach people from a somewhat different culture than people in our church?

The primary focus of Samaria, from a "God-Sized Vision" perspective, is partnering with other churches culturally different from yours to help them prevail in their ministry to their community and varied demographic. Since most churches have migrated to the suburbs in recent decades, an initial focus for Samaria would likely be the inner city.

Our home campus is located in the suburbs of Greater Dayton. Although we are located on a primary interstate highway at the edge OF our city, we don't believe our address absolves us of a sense of responsibility FOR our city. As such, at Christian Life Center, we have about ten inner city partner churches that comprise our "Samaria" focus.

Realistically, we know that most people in our urban center will never travel to CLC to attend church. It is just impractical to do so. So, we partner with churches all across our inner city with the goal of lifting their ministry up to reach people in their neighborhoods, to make a difference for Christ's sake.

Our goal is NOT to lift up our church's name in the urban community; it is to lift up our partner churches to be noticed by the residents of their surrounding neighborhood

Some examples may help you visualize what may be possible in your area. Each summer we try to do a major outreach "offensive" with our partner churches. We insist in not doing it *for* them, but *with* them. To do so we have co-hosted many "outreach block parties." These festive events are complete with kids' games, face painting, health services, and a prayer station for any needs. We send volunteers from our congregation to work with our partners.

The day is filled with food, music, fun, and compassion. Seldom, if ever, do guests know that CLC is assisting and helping to financially sponsor the event. Our goal is not to get our church's name in the community, but instead to lift up our partner churches to be noticed by residents in their surrounding neighborhood.

We also partner in other ways. For example, one of our partner churches felt led to target reaching children in their neighborhood (as part of reaching their Jerusalem). One of our adult groups mobilized about a dozen artistic and construction volunteers to do an extreme makeover of an unused room in the partner church. They did a "Disney-quality" job of providing this church with a state-of-the-art kids' space. The room included a lighted puppet stage in front of a giant flat screen monitor, all on a raised platform in a room with painted walls that looked "AWESOME" (as some of the 7 year olds declared).

> We want our partner churches to be seen as a source of help and compassion in their neighborhoods. Knowing they are a blessing to their "Jerusalem" is blessing enough for us.

Thanksgiving also provides a great opportunity for us to partner together to reach our Samaria. For the past many years, our congregation raises funds and grocery donations to provide a Thanksgiving meal for 1,500 to 2,000 families (depending on need any given year). We put a frozen turkey along with all the trimmings in a box and distribute them throughout our city.

Of the recipients, less than 400 of those families come to our Little York location to pick up their food. While with us, we provide a simple lunch (hot dogs, sandwiches), a Gospel presentation, and an opportunity to pray for needs our guests may have. Caring and friendly hosts guide recipients through the process, helping strangers to leave feeling like friends. Many make a decision to follow Christ as a result.

The other 1,100 to 1,600 boxes are distributed through our partner churches. It is so encouraging to tour our partners during distribution day. Small churches get long lines (often extending out their doors) of people eager to receive this compassionate holiday provision. Again, we don't tell these people this is a gift from CLC. As far as they know, the partner church is providing this to them. We want our partner churches to be seen as a source of help and compassion in their neighborhoods. Knowing they are a blessing to their "Jerusalem" is blessing enough for us!

You may notice one of the examples I didn't give for our work with our Samaria and our partner churches. We don't give financial resources to help them "stay afloat," so-to-speak. As such, we don't pay light bills or mortgages to help struggling inner-city churches stay open. *We believe that if God wants a church to exist, and the pastor is being obedient in preaching and leadership, God will provide the essentials.*

However, beyond ongoing expenses of staying open if a repair is needed on the building itself (because we see the facility as a tool to help with the work of ministry) we often help. Still, our main focus isn't facility repair. We see our partnership as a way to help inner-city partner congregations "go on offense" to reach their community. If they have a genuine need to help them reach out, we are usually interested.

> Our desire is simply to be "wind beneath their wings." We want to provide additional volunteers, and financial resources, to help our partners prevail in their community.

For example, a few years ago as the end of our fiscal year arrived, we realized over the last half of the year, that we had received $500,000 additional offerings in our general fund. This presented a great "God-sized opportunity" for us. Of the total excess we designated $75,000 to go toward our partner churches. The requirement was that the funds were to be used in some kind of outreach need that the church couldn't do otherwise. We offered each of our partner churches a $5,000 outreach grant if they submitted an appropriate request. What a joy to be able to say "yes" to help under-resourced churches with a vision to reach their community! The rest of the $500,000 we gave away by investing it in compassionate outreach ministries around the globe.

It was exciting to contact missionaries we supported and ask them to send a request for up to $30,000 to do something that would expand the impact of their ministry that they couldn't do if they didn't receive this unexpected financial gift. We have found that the God-Sized Vision tends to bring resources and opportunities we, and our partners around the globe, didn't expect!

One last thing to keep in mind, *this is a partnership*. As such, our board asks partner churches to contribute something toward the cost of our efforts together ("skin-in-the-game," so to speak). Typically, we ask for at least 10% of the cost of a project. Recently when we replaced a boiler, the partner church paid about 25% of the cost and we provided 75%. The added savings in repairs and utilities can now be used by our partner on an ongoing basis to help this church fund their overall mission.

A common theme we tell our partners is that we don't want to tell them what their vision should be. They need to prayerfully **discern**, **define**, **declare** and **do** the vision for their church. Our desire is to simply be "wind beneath their wings." We want to provide additional volunteers and financial resources to help our partners prevail in their community. It is a tremendous joy to hear their stories of how God is using our relationship to encourage them and grow their ministry.

> A common theme we tell our partners is that we don't want to tell them what their vision should be. THEY need to prayerfully **discern**, **define**, **declare** and **do** the vision for their church.

You may be struggling with "Where do we start?" If your Samaria is your urban center, you may be overwhelmed with the complexity and magnitude of problems ranging from inter-generational poverty, crime, education system issues, drug abuse, and the list goes on and on.

For starters, you may want a healthy frame of reference by first reading the book *Toxic Charity* by Robert Lupton.[8] Unfortunately, churches have a history of trying to help in dire situations, but in the long run, end up enabling the very problems they hoped to solve. The words of Jesus speak to us across the centuries of time, "I was hungry and you fed me...naked and you clothed me..." The church must be compassionately involved in works of "Matthew 25" basic Christian compassion.

Due to government intervention through welfare programs, the plight of the poor and their needs is more complicated than in Jesus' day. We must indeed care for the basic needs of the poor around us, while tending to them in a way that facilitates helping them discover and live the productive Christian life that God intended for them. This is far more involved and difficult than providing "handouts" to the needy. *While such compassion may feel good to the giver at the moment, if we are going to truly help those in need it is going to require a longer term strategic investment of time, talent, and treasures than the average church has realized in the past.*

Our intent is partnership that helps make a long term difference. We didn't start out with 10 partners. We didn't begin with large financial investments. We made many mistakes along the way. There are many challenges, and to be honest, I understand why most churches don't get involved cross-culturally. It's not easy. If you are just venturing in to a "Samaria" focus, try finding one church that you can begin a very limited partnership kind of relationship with and let it grow over time, learning from it as you go. We have been "partnering" and learning together with inner-city churches for almost twenty years!

Don't let the complexity of the task and size of the need deter you from making a difference in your Samaria. Jesus commanded us to it, so our only true answer is "Yes Lord" perhaps followed by a "Now what?"

---

[8] Robert Lupton. (2011). *Toxic Charity*: *How Churches and Charities Hurt Those They Help, and How to Reverse it*. New York, NY: Harper Collins.

Questions for consideration:

1. Prayerfully reflect on your congregation. List five adjectives that describe the dominant demographic characteristics of your church. (Age, race, economics, residency, etc.)

   _____

   _____

   _____

   _____

2. What kind of congregations could you reach out to that minister to people culturally different from your congregation? What characteristics would make them a cross cultural/Samaria kind of church for you?

   _____

   _____

   _____

   _____

3. Note: For this next exercise, based on our experience at Christian Life Center, I would recommend that every suburban church applying this book reach out to an inner city urban church, either in your immediate area or in the closest urban center.

   Brainstorm and list three small projects or activities your church and a potential "Samaria" partner church could do together that would help you get to know each other, while at the same time, serve the community of this potential partner church.

   _____

   _____

   _____

   _____

   _____

   _____

Chapter Eleven: Defining Our "Uttermost Parts of the Earth"

Little did the first followers of Christ realize that the Gospel would be spread from Israel all the way to the United States. As far as we know, they didn't even know there was a United States (Granted, the nation was born centuries later, but the land mass was there!). I'm thankful that God knew, and that in His providence, as an American, I would come to know the Good News of Jesus Christ through their obedience to the initial "God-Sized Vision."

The question regarding the "uttermost-part" of your God-Sized Vision is:

What ministry can we partner with to make an evangelistic and "Matthew 25" kind of difference in another part of the world?

Many would call this "foreign missions." For the average church, a non-God-Sized Vision approach means sending some amount of monthly financial support to a missionary or foreign relief agency. As we have come to know our call to the "uttermost parts of the world," I would suggest that this kind of response is only a part of your God-Sized Vision.

> Historically, it seems the church has done one or the other, caring for the spiritual and ignoring the physical, or vice-versa. James 2:14-20 makes it clear that it is not "either/or," but rather "both/and."

In my years of ministry, I have found that God has consistently guided us to attend to the needs of "the least of these" as cited in Matthew 25. There, in verses 31-46, Jesus underscores the importance of what I call "basic Christian compassion." This involves meeting the needs of those who are hungry, thirsty, in need of clothing and shelter, sick and in prison, etc. *I believe EVERY church should be able to show how they provide basic Christian compassion to those in need, both in their Samaria, and in some area of the "uttermost parts" of the world.*

At the same time, you will notice in the "uttermost-parts" question that we are to make both a compassionate and an evangelistic impact. Historically, it seems the church has done one or the other, caring for spiritual and ignoring the physical, or vice-versa. James 2:14-20 makes it clear that it is not "either/or," but rather "both/and."

When we launched the "God-Sized Vision," it created a calling for me and our church. This led us to a small country that I honestly didn't know anything about before this journey began. If you would have asked me, I wouldn't have known where to tell you to find it on a map. Like the original disciples and America, I was totally unfamiliar with that "uttermost part" of the world as we started our journey.

That was six trips ago. Now, as I write this, I'm anticipating yet another trip to Swaziland, Africa, a country of about 1 million people on the northeast border of the country of South Africa. Poverty and AIDS are ravaging this tiny nation the size of New Jersey. It is estimated that 75 percent of Swazi's live on less than a dollar a day, and the World Health Organization fears the HIV infection rate could threaten the very existence of this country in the coming decades.

It is to this land that we believe God has called us. Through an amazing chain of events that would take too long to document in this book, we found a partner in Swaziland with a vision for transformation (On second thought, for this story, please refer to the chapter in the

> If you would have asked me, I wouldn't have known where to tell you to find it on a map. Like the original disciples and America, I was totally unfamiliar with that "Uttermost part" of the world as we started our journey.

APPENDIX telling how God opened up one of the greatest doors of ministry our church has ever known. He can do it for you too!).

Consistent with our work in our Samaria, this vision depends on partnerships that encourage the vitality of the local church. We are pursuing a strategy of bringing change "In the Community, By the Community" with holistic ministry of a local church at the center of it. We call it "ICBC."

We start by partnering with a community-minded pastor and build a church, a home for the pastor, and an additional home or two for a widow to live in and provide care for some of the most disadvantaged orphans from these rural African communities (20 percent of the population of Swaziland consists of orphans under the age of 21). Beyond these residential opportunities, other church members are trained to do community outreach and care for orphans struggling to live on their own but who are not living in one of the ICBC homes. We also provide animals and gardens to help make the church self-sustaining within two years of opening.

God used Bono, lead singer of U2, in an interview with Bill Hybels at a Willow Creek Association Leadership Summit, to "seal the deal" so-to-speak.

Since construction is far more basic than in the U.S., we are able to build these transformational communities for about $150,000 each. Sustainability funds require about another $20,000 a year for the first two years (This includes a small salary for the pastor, who must find a way to generate income after the first two years).

What excites me is to have someone who recently returned from a mission trip to one of our "ICBC's" stop me in a local grocery store. Their response is typical of people we send to Swaziland, *Pastor Stan, it is working!* ICBC is really making a difference for these wonderful people!" And so the story goes.

The initial vision of our partner in Swaziland for the ICBC approach to community transformation was that eventually Swaziland would become the "pulpit to Africa." Lord willing, the upcoming trip I'm taking is one of discovery. We have built three "ICBC" communities in Swaziland in the past 5 years with plans and financing for two more already "in the cue." We plan to travel to Zambia in anticipation of launching the first ICBC across the continent of Africa (See update in appendix). We sense that we will continue to plant "ICBC" communities in Swaziland until we have built as many as 60 in the next 25 years. In addition, we hope to plant three in each country we venture into beyond Swaziland, and see where God takes it from there (The APPENDIX article on Swaziland provides information on how interested churches can join us in this work).

Let me say that in no way did I imagine we would be doing something of this magnitude when the God-Sized Vision first began. For many years, I had no desire whatsoever to be involved in, or even travel to Africa. When we did begin to feel called to this continent, God used Bono, lead singer of U2, in an interview with Bill Hybels at a Willow Creek Leadership Summit, to "seal the deal" so-to-speak.

This compelling interview basically found this rock icon calling out the American church. Bono rightly cited that poverty and AIDS were ravaging the continent of Africa, and as of 2005, other than some relief organizations, the church had hardly showed up. This "push" was the confirmation we needed, and the rest is history.

> I believe our involvement in Africa has captured the heart and "pocketbook" of our church family. We are forever grateful for the opportunity, and we will never be the same.

Now, our partnership with Swaziland is an integral part of our church's DNA. As noted earlier, we have invested over $1.7 million in our Swaziland initiatives over the past five years, and we see no end in sight. Nor would we want to. I believe our involvement in Africa has captured the heart and "pocketbook" of our church family. We are forever grateful for the opportunity, and we will never be the same. Personally, while 20 hours in a coach seat (I'm 6'3" tall) all the way to Africa isn't pleasant, I am eager for each trip I take.

I've joked with our partner in Swaziland, "You're the most expensive friend I've ever had." While kidding, it's true. And I couldn't be more grateful for our relationship. *God has breathed a sense of life into our church, not by living in church survival mode or by hoarding, and taking care of ourselves, but by giving and "spending ourselves" for others in our God-Sized Vision that He is calling us to.*

I've shared this journey to encourage you that God likely has exciting and rewarding plans for you in the "uttermost parts of the world" that you aren't even aware of yet. The first step is in stepping out!

As with each dimension of the God-Sized Vision, it is the responsibility of leadership to **Discern, Define, Declare** and **Do** the vision. *Discerning our next step in the "uttermost parts" required us to ask questions beyond the existing missions program of our church.* Since our church began in 1968, we have always been a supporter of foreign missions. We currently give financial support to over 100 missionaries and relief agencies. *In stepping in to the God-Sized Vision dimension of your church, we don't suggest that you stop any support of missionaries, but rather that you re-think your next choices.*

A God-Sized Vision approach to foreign missions involves more than financial support and the occasional project or mission trip.

...the question to ask is, "Where can we begin?" I suggest you begin with baby-steps; learn and grow. After all, the Biblical principle to follow is this: Be faithful over little. Learn and grow, and God will lead you to be faithful over much. (Matthew 25: 21, 23)

Consistent with an Acts 1:8 approach to vision, we believe we must have at least one "Partnership" kind of relationship in the "uttermost parts" of the Earth, with ministry that puts the local church along with "Matthew 25 compassion" at the focal point.

Admittedly, the kind of partnership we developed requires finances and people that many churches may not be able to afford as they begin this journey. Start small, learn, and the vision will grow. As with all aspects of the God-Sized Vision, the question to ask is "Where can we begin?" I suggest you begin with baby-steps, learn, and grow. *After all, the Biblical principle to follow is this: Be faithful over little. Learn and grow, and God will lead you to be faithful over much.* (Matthew 25:21, 23)

Perhaps your church can start by selecting one of the missionaries you already support who does much of their work in or through local churches. Ask yourself, "How can we develop this support into more of a partnership relationship that will increase their impact through their local (uttermost part) church?" Or, you may go on a mission of discovery, as we did, for a fresh start in an area of new calling for your congregation.

If you lead a smaller church, or one with very limited resources, the best place to start is to enhance an existing relationship. Communication with your current missionary is essential. Find one who wants more engagement with your congregation. Perhaps you simply start with regular updates from them which are met with a prayer response from your church. Today's media tools and

> You may feel overwhelmed with this idea and not sure where to start. That's actually GREAT! In our weakness, God can show His true strength. When we are not totally sure of our steps, we are most dependent on God's guidance.

the internet make everything from "sound-bites" to photographic or film clip updates much easier to obtain than in the past.

To really make the partnership serious, find tangible ways to further invest in this ministry as a purposeful relationship. Again, prioritize those investments of prayer, money, and people that will either meet "Matthew 25" needs, or enhance the evangelistic ministry of the local church, and preferably, both!

You may feel overwhelmed with this idea and not sure where to start. That's actually great! In our weakness God can show His true strength. When we are not totally sure of our steps, we are most dependent on God's guidance. Chances are that as you prayerfully take your first "baby steps," they will be directed by God, for His glory, and for your good. I doubt Peter had a lot of confidence on how to walk on water or where to take his first "aqua-steps." *The key is that in not knowing, He did it anyway!*

Let me add one more helpful thought here. We aren't doing the "ICBC" approach with all our 100 missionaries, just one. We continue to support the others. We often feature these different missionaries before our congregation for their continued prayer and financial support. But the unique God-Sized Vision partnership relationship requires us to have intense focus. We have an "ICBC" ministry with our Swaziland partners, and give a disproportionate amount of time and finances to it, because we discern God has called us to this.

> There are so many good things to do that churches can make the mistake of saying "yes" to everything and make a substantive difference in nothing.

In "Church work," it is easy to get distracted or to be spread "a mile wide and an inch deep." There are so many good things to do that churches can make the mistake of saying "yes" to everything and make a substantive difference in nothing. So, for us, we are glad to give monthly support to missionaries and relief agencies that aren't our "ICBC" partner. Still, at the present time God isn't calling us to go further with them, nor do we have the time, resources, or conviction to do so.

We are learning to be focused and obedient to what God has called us to focus on. We are finding that in doing so, God is doing more than we ever imagined and our non-partnership ministries are still blessed and appreciative of our traditional support. I believe God is eager to guide you to involvement of greater impact in international ministry through your church. It has been part of His plan since Jesus gave the vision recorded in Acts 1:8. As you pursue it, a step at a time, the vision will grow as you'll learn. And trust me, you and your people will be changed by what happens.

Get started!

Questions for consideration:

1. Prayerfully review the list of foreign missionaries your church currently supports. Ask the Holy Spirit to prompt your heart toward those who might be the most likely partners to get more involved with. Write down their names and the countries they serve. If your church currently does not support any foreign missionaries, take a globe (or world map), pray over it, and ask God to impress areas of the world (whether it be single countries, or entire continents) on your heart for potential future focus. Now, write them down.-

   _____

   _____

   Note: When you share and discuss this in a group setting with your church leaders/staff, write down any missionaries or places that are cited by more than one leader. This may be a starting point.

   _____

   _____

   _____

2. Do some brief research, either online or with the missionary you are thinking of, about the needs facing this nation/part of the world. List as many as you discover: physical, economic, social, spiritual, political, relational, etc. Again, the emphasis at this time is brief. There will be a time for in-depth research once you clearly **discern** who your first international partner will be.

   _____

   _____

   _____

3. If you currently support missionaries, a first step in **defining** your approach may be to decide what are three small things you could **do** as a church to focus on at least one missionary to enhance your relationship?_____

   _____

   _____

Chapter Twelve: Perspective

The purpose of this book so far has been to help show the simple "Vision template" that Jesus left to His first disciples to follow and to realize that it holds true as a pattern for us still today. When guided by Acts 1:8, the church both now just as then, will embark on a "God-Sized Vision" that truly makes a difference.

This book has tried to help "put flesh" on the Acts 1:8 template. The questions for consideration at the end of each chapter have been designed to get church leaders thinking in this kind of direction. They have also been geared to starting small. Too often vision dies at birth when "too big" thoughts overwhelm those who sincerely want to step out, but they resign, unsure of "what, how, when, or where."

> Too often vision dies at birth, when "too big" thoughts overwhelm those who sincerely want to step out, but they resign, unsure of "what, how, when, or where."

As pastors, staff, or lay leaders read this book and complete the questions, I believe their hearts will already sense an awakening to a desire for vision opportunities. If you take it a step further by turning each chapter into a time of group sharing and prayer, with someone assigned to be the scribe keeping track of key themes and promptings, I believe seeds of future direction will begin to be planted in your hearts as exciting next steps will begin to unfold.

Take some time to review and pray about the chapters you've just read and answered questions about. In a **discerning** mode, with a "God-Sized Vision" orientation to Acts 1:8, there are more practical questions for you to answer. Use the following questions as a starting point to define what you might begin to **do** in **defining** your God-Sized Vision.

1. **Jerusalem**: What should our key priorities be, at this season, to enhance the **spiritual vitality** of our congregation?

   _____

   _____

   _____

   _____

2. **Judea:** What initial steps can we take to support the cause of **church multiplication** somewhere in our region?

   _____

   _____

   _____

   _____

3. **Samaria:** What congregation (or, what kind of congregation) in our area or extended region, can we begin a **partnership** with to enhance their ministry to **people our church doesn't typically reach**? Whenever possible/appropriate, Matthew 25 compassion should be included. Likewise, whenever possible, it is highly suggested that suburban churches seek urban partners.

   _____

   _____

   _____

   _____

4. **Uttermost Parts of the Earth:** Where, and with whom, can we begin to develop an **intentional international partnership** with to enhance their impact on that part of the world, including the cause of Matthew 25 "Basic Christian compassion" along with evangelism?

   _____

   _____

   _____

   _____

Principles To Follow:

There are some basic principles to keep in mind as you pursue a "God-Sized Vision." A few are listed below for consideration. Please read the verses mentioned, jot down your thoughts/reactions, and then discuss it with your group.

1. **The Matthew 25: 21, 23 principle: Faithful over little/faithful over much.** Throughout the years, I am learning it is usually better to dream big, **discern** much, and then start small. As you begin to **do** your God-Sized Vision, take "baby steps" of faith. God will honor these steps and open the next doors for you to go through.

   > I am learning it is usually better to dream big, discern much, and then start small.

   Notice, the two talent servant didn't start with four, nor did the five talent servant start with ten; and I assume they didn't end with four or ten either! Be patient, be intentional, step out, do well, trust God, and grow with it!

   Notes:_____
   _____
   _____
   _____
   _____
   _____

2. **The Luke 14:27-34 principle: The cost of discipleship.**
   The obvious lesson learned from the fool who started to build a tower but then ran out of resources is to do "due diligence" in planning your steps. You'll recall that it took us from February until September before our God-Sized Vision was ready to go from **Discern** and **Define**, to **Declare.** As such, be patient, intentional, and "thorough enough" (I say

"thorough enough" because some get so immersed in details that the vision gets lost due to the "paralysis of analysis.")

However, the original intent of the parable of the talents was more about sacrificing our possessions for the call of discipleship (see verse 33). As such, be prepared that as you venture into **discerning** the God-Sized Vision in store for you it will likely cost you in many ways. The way you spend your time, energy, finances, and even your priorities will change (Please see the Appendix for how we decided to fund the vision at our church. I totally recommend it).

> The way you spend your time, energy, finances, and even your priorities will change.

Notes:_____

_____

_____

_____

_____

_____

_____

_____

_____

_____

3. **The 2 Corinthians 5:9-10 principle: God is an accountability God.** Someday, according to this verse, we will all stand before the judgment seat of Christ and answer an amazing question. I picture Jesus to ask it something like this: "Stan, I left heaven, took on the form of a man, was born in a barn, lived an unappreciated life, died a death I didn't deserve, was buried in a grave, and rose from the dead to purchase your eternal life."

"In addition to that, when you accepted me as your Lord and Savior, I sent my Holy Spirit to dwell in you. You were given spiritual gifts for the work of ministry. You were given resources, opportunities, and a life that no one else had quite the same as you. In addition to all that, I have been preparing a place here, in heaven, for you."

Then, I imagine a look of knowing anticipation in Jesus' eyes as He asks the question, "Stan, what did you do for me, with all that I have given to you?"

1 Corinthians 3:10-15 makes it clear that we as Christians won't be judged for our sins, but we will be rewarded according to what we did for Christ's sake. My prayer is that someday I'll hear Him say, "Well done," as will every person pursuing a God-Sized Vision for their church and for their personal life. Notes:_____

_____
_____
_____
_____
_____
_____
_____

> I imagine a look of knowing anticipation in Jesus' eyes as He asks, "What did you do for me, with all that I have given to you?"

4. **The Acts 20:35 principle: Seek to give, more than get.**

This verse, along with Matthew 6:19-21, makes it clear—our focus should be more on giving than getting. It is impossible to study the call of Christ to His followers and not understand that it is meant to be a life of sacrifice ("Take up your cross," "Lose your life to find it," etc.). How could we expect His expectations for the collective body of individual Christians in the church to be any different?

It is understandable to wonder where the money, time, and talent are going to come from to pursue a "God-Sized Vision" for your church.

Don't let this lack of resources keep you from saying "Yes!" Jesus called followers before telling them how it was going to all work out. He didn't tell Matthew or Peter how they would make ends meet once they abandoned their careers. He called them, they followed, and Christ provided.

Make no mistake about it, a "God-Sized Vision" is costly….in every way. But I have learned that what God calls you to, He provides for. So many churches are afraid to launch out into a "new vision, thinking they can't afford it since they barely have enough resources to get by. Sadly, they fail to realize the lack of a God-Sized Vision is exactly why they barely get by. I have found that people want to give and dedicate themselves in support of something bigger than them. *The church was never meant to be in "survival mode."*

> Jesus didn't tell Matthew or Peter how they would make ends meet once they abandoned their careers. He called, they followed, Christ provided.

If the gates of hell can't prevail against us (the church), then struggling economies, adverse cultural conditions, risky ministry endeavors, or a lack of prior "Big Vision" experience can't either! God blesses us to be a blessing. Trust Him in this and you'll see.

Notes:_____

_____

_____

_____

_____

5. **The Hebrews 12 Principle: No risk, no faith.** The entire chapter of Hebrews 12 has been an inspiration to Christ-followers throughout history. In it, we are inspired by Godly risk-takers. Throughout Biblical history, men and women are celebrated who were bold enough to trust God for the impossible: Noah built an ark (having never even seen a ship before) and literally saved humanity. Sarah gave birth to the promised ancestral lineage of Jesus himself at 90 years of age. Fugitive Moses returned to the Egyptian empire to lead an entire enslaved nation to freedom (after four centuries of slavery.) The list goes on and on.

    Notice, none of these heroes are celebrated for doing ordinary things. They were indeed ordinary people, but they did *extraordinary* things for God. The key is at the start of the chapter. They did these "impossible" things, through faith, an unshakeable assurance of hope, and a conviction of God's unseen vision becoming reality.

    > Throughout Biblical history, men and women are celebrated who were bold enough to trust God for the impossible!

    There is nothing in Scripture to indicate that God has any different expectations for us today than for His followers of the past. We are to do great things for Him. Just as Daniel (11:32b) declared this centuries ago, it is still true today.

    We revere Bible heroes because they took risks for God's sake, so let's be the kind of people of faith who inspire others who will remember us. Now more than ever before the church needs to rise up in faith to do great things for God's sake.

    Let those who observe or remember us do so and be challenged because we too took leaps of faith to do things too great for us to accomplish without faith in a God who leads, guides, and provides. As the first generation of Christ-followers said "Yes" to the daunting call to take Christ to their Jerusalem, Judea, Samaria, and on to the uttermost-parts of the Earth, let us do the same. The challenges are great, the rewards even greater, and the thrill of the journey is "God-Sized" to match the vision!

Notes:_____

_____

_____

_____

_____

_____

Chapter Thirteen: Now What?

In the pages of this brief book, I've tried to explain how you can use Acts 1:8 as a template for a new and compelling "God-Sized Vision" for your church. Too often, churches only focus on the first half of that verse, rightly citing that the Holy Spirit is given to empower us, but then fail to emphasize what we empowered to do.

Indeed the Holy Spirit does empower us. However, this empowerment is not just so we can feel good in a worship service or so we get our spiritual tank filled to simply cope with another week of life. There is a purpose behind the work of the Holy Spirit in our lives. The Holy Spirit dwells within every believer and gives each of us spiritual gifts for the work of ministry, and indeed empowers us to be witnesses for Christ. He has been given to us to make a difference for Christ's sake.

> Draw it out. Put your headings across the top, draw your four columns, and begin to chart a course toward a well **discerned** and **defined** vision, which will be clearly **declared**, and then **done**!

How sad and frustrating it must be to God for churches to focus on the presence and gifts of the Holy Spirit within those who follow Christ as though it is just to provide an 'abundant life' to Christians, while ignoring the Acts 1:8 reason the Holy Spirit has been given to us in the first place. Such misplaced emphasis yields disappointed Christians and ineffective churches. Promoting the idea within the church that the Holy Spirit is only given to Christians for their own good is like telling soldiers their weapons are only for target practice and that the army is not for protecting a nation. It misses the point entirely!

The Holy Spirit has been given to us so that we might have the power to be witnesses for Christ. First, we are to be witnesses in the area we live (Jerusalem), with the people we work with, go to school with, live near. Next, we are to reach out and spread the

Gospel to a surrounding, extended geographic area by, if at all possible, helping with the process of church multiplication. Third, we are to take this same message cross-culturally to those in need. Finally, we must take the Gospel to foreign lands, to people and cultures different and distant to our own, all in the name of Christ.

Use the prayerful discussions meant to be prompted by this book, and the notes you've written as the starting point for your own "God-Sized Vision." Put your heading across the top, draw your four columns, and begin to chart a course toward a well **discerned** and **defined** vision, which will be clearly **declared**, and then **done**! This will bring glory to God, and those who join in will be extremely glad they did.

Building the Church, Changing our World, a "God-Sized Vision" for_____Acts 1:8

(Our) Jerusalem	Judea	Samaria	Uttermost Parts

APPENDIX ONE: FUNDING THE GOD-SIZED VISION

When we embarked on the God-Sized Vision for our church, we knew it would take resources. Such a vision would require us to prioritize spending our time, energy, and finances as a church.

We debated how to financially account for these new endeavors: should we add such funds to our existing chart of accounts? Was it a new department? How do we handle both income and expenditures to our new vision?

We decided to set up a separate fund simply called "The God-Sized Vision Fund" for efforts reaching our Judea, Samaria, and the Uttermost Parts of the World. It is from this fund that we pay for building ICBC's (Uttermost Parts), Inner city partnership efforts (Samaria), and launching new satellite congregations across greater Dayton (Judea). While we don't use the fund for operational aspects of our Jerusalem ministry (for us that is what our church budget is for), we do use the God-Sized Vision fund for actual expansions of our facilities at our Jerusalem (Little York Road Campus).

Having completed five years in our journey, we are now up to the point where we budget approximately 20% of our general fund giving (tithes) to go to the God-Sized Vision. For us, this amounts to $1 million a year. This is in addition to over $600,000 that is given toward our "Missions and Outreach Ministries" fund. Overall, about 24% of the money we receive goes either to the needs of the "God-Sized Vision" or to missionaries and relief agencies we support in our outreach fund.

When we first returned from our initial trip to Swaziland, Africa I remember preaching a message about our finances. I had a stack of $1 bills and counted out two piles. The first pile, I would count out 24 bills, then put $1 in the other pile. I did it over and over, until I had counted out $100. There was $96 in the larger pile and $4 in the small one. Sadly, at that time, the small pile represented how much of our total giving was spent outside our walls, and beyond our local community, only 4%. You can imagine how thankful we are to see that change so dramatically in only 5 years.

We set aside money for the God-Sized Vision to keep us intentional. We also set it aside to make it easier to monitor what we are doing toward each area. It is amazing to see how God has blessed this approach to stewardship. As noted earlier, from the God-Sized Vision Fund we have been able to purchase four "ICBC" communities in Africa (with others planned). We have been able to launch three multi-sites from our Little York Campus in the greater Dayton area. We have invested heavily in our inner city partner churches. And we have built a 30,000 square foot addition at our Little York Campus, and paid cash. We are also currently in the process of expanding our original sanctuary...part of the original vision drawn in 2008 (see the lower left hand corner of the drawing.)

I don't know how typical these results will be for your church, but I can say that throughout my years as a lead pastor (since 1990), I have consistently seen that God provides funds when we practice "Mathew 25" compassion. When we have extra money in our general fund (tithes) at the end of the fiscal year (and it happens more often than not), we try to give much, if not all, of it away generously. We invest it in God-Sized Vision related ministries or in missionaries and relief agencies we support.

> I have reminded our leadership countless times, "It takes a lot of hard work to spend money well."

I was raised with a saying, "You can't out-give God." We find that to be true year after year.

So, decide how you are going to "put your money where your mouth is" when it comes to financing your "God-Sized Vision" and get started. As noted throughout this book, I recommend you begin small, intentionally, and grow it over time.

Decide ahead of time what you are willing to invest (spend) in each of the categories (Jerusalem, Judea, etc.). We put an upper "lid" on the amount. The following statement is a good example: "We invest up to $120,000 a year in our Samaria partner churches." This expresses intent, adds some accountability, and also helps avoid spending for spending's sake, just to meet an obligatory target. I have reminded our leadership countless times, "It takes a lot of hard work to spend money well."

APPENDIX TWO: THE SWAZILAND STORY

Around 2005, I felt God began to deal with me about the lack of impact our church was having in Africa in spite of the fact that AIDS and poverty were ravaging the entire continent. It seems other people throughout our church were raising similar concerns as the question began to come up repeatedly, "Is there any opportunity for our church to get involved in Africa?"

We had attempted to get started about five years before that. We partnered with a group that built "Tabernacle churches" in an equatorial African country (Tabernacle churches are simply a concrete slab with metal frame and a corrugated metal roof, no sides, nothing fancy). We sent several teams, built 4 or 5 of the structures, but a relationship never really developed with the missionaries we built for. We just never seemed to connect.

Then, at the Willow Creek Association Leadership Summit in 2006, Bono was interviewed by Bill Hybels, and the rest is history. As soon as the interview was completed and that session of the Summit was taking a break, lay leaders began to speak up and show interest, "If CLC ever gets involved in Africa."

I asked our missions staff person to do some prayerful research. His task was to identify potential partnership countries. The criteria were:

1. AIDS and poverty must be key problems.
2. The country must be relatively politically stable
3. We wanted a country small enough that our efforts wouldn't seem like a drop in the bucket
4. If possible, English speaking would be a "plus" for teams we might send

We met about a month later, and he simply said, "Based on the criteria, and prayer, I'd say Swaziland is the place!" After more prayer and consideration, in December of 2007, 6 other "CLC'ers" and I were on our way to Swaziland, Africa. I told our congregation we were going on an exploratory trip to Africa, "To find a community we can partner with, build a church, and do holistic ministry. We want to have a relationship so that we can see this community change over time."

Looking back, I had no idea how naively optimistic that claim was. Our plans were simply to go look around Swaziland; a missionary was going to host us, showing us around the little nation of 1 million people, the size of Rhode Island. Looking back, there was no way that trip, as planned, was going to yield a conclusive partner for us. As it ended up, the missionary planned to do what he normally does with groups from big American churches. He showed us several unfinished, worthy projects that we could give money toward. We might even send a missions team to help with construction needs on the project.

However, when we were done, that is all it would amount to—a project. A project that we "threw money at," a project that we indeed helped finish, but a project, not a partnership. We felt called to so much more.

So, let's back up to the trip itself. I will never forget the seven of us sitting in the Detroit airport, waiting for our second of three flights on the itinerary, when a friend of mine with Book of Hope texted me from Florida. His text read something like: "Hey Stan, in Swaziland, try to connect with a guy named Kevin Ward. He is a strategic thinker and I believe you will hit it off with him." I chuckled and told our group, "OK, I'm supposed to keep an eye out for a guy named Kevin Ward." This instruction sounded a little like finding a needle in a haystack as the team lightheartedly gave me an "ok, sure" and that was the end of it.

The next day we landed in Africa (without our luggage, not unusual), and the trip began. Our missionary host met us, got us checked in our place of lodging, and we began the first of several tours to fundable projects. While we were indeed fascinated with our drive through the Swaziland countryside, it wasn't what we were looking for. The next evening we were booked for dinner at the missionary's home.

Unfortunately, all the national leaders of the denomination we were working with were out of the country the week we were there, except for the treasurer. He had called our host three days before our arrival, with an offer something like: "Hey, I know you have a group coming from the United States, and all the officers are out of the country. If you need any help driving them around or hosting them, let me know and I'll make myself available to help."

Our missionary host thanked him for the offer and said, "I'm having them over to our home for dinner. Since you are a native Swazi, why don't you join us? You can tell them about the culture, and share whatever is on your heart." Kevin Ward accepted that invitation, and providence happened!

That evening, you can imagine the look on my face as I not only met Kevin Ward, but then introduced him and his wife Helen to our team. After dinner, we sat and listened to his astute grasp on Swazi culture and his conviction that transformation must come from In the Community, By the Community, with a holistic church at the center of it (Hence, ICBC)! After several conversations with Kevin during the final days of our trip, the partnership was born.

Our farewell meeting was over breakfast at the Mountain Inn in the capital city of Mbabane. He gave us an estimated budget of what it would cost to build a church, pastor's home, and a duplex that would house a widow who could raise 6-10 orphans (Think James 1:27). We pledged our passionate interest and headed back to CLC mid-December of 2007 to help begin what would become part of the "God-Sized Vision" to be launched during the next two to nine months after we returned.

> If your church would like to learn about partnering with us to help build ICBC's in Africa, we would love to connect with you.

As mentioned in the text of this book, we have launched 3 ICBC's since that time, with two more in the planning stages, and another in Zambia about to begin. It costs approximately $125-150,000 to build the church, pastor's home, and children's home duplex, if significant amounts of volunteer labor (both locals and mission trip participants) can be included. This establishes the actual site after we have identified the right pastor for the place (an important connection, whether in Africa or America!). Then, we pay up to $24,000 a year for the first two years to assist with expenses to get the ICBC economically self-sufficient.

After the initial two years, our relationship shifts from including financial provision, to being primarily ministry related (sending various outreach and discipleship teams), or focused on enhancing the impact and scope of the church (we often add a cabin to the sites to help them host visiting teams, etc.).

If your church would like to join us in this partnership, we would love to connect with you. Please visit our website at clcdayton.com, click on the Swaziland link, and follow it to the place for partnership opportunities. Someone will get in touch with you.

ZAMBIA UPDATE: Since beginning the draft for this book, as mentioned earlier, I travelled to Zambia and Swaziland along with another member of our leadership team. In addition to visiting the three "ICBC" communities in Swaziland that we have helped launch, we identified a fourth to begin in the coming months, and potentially a fifth that could begin this year as well.

Our trip to Zambia confirmed that we are indeed ready to launch an "ICBC" there. Our partner will be the pastor who was the key assistant for Kevin Ward in Swaziland for ten years. His visa expired almost three years ago. Our disappointment over him having to return home to Zambia turned out to be Romans 8:28 in the making! This pastor, perfectly trained in the ICBC model, will now begin this ministry in the first country outside of Swaziland.

APPENDIX THREE: THE LUKE COMMISSION

Visit the Luke Commission's website to learn about this amazing medical ministry to Africa, beginning in Swaziland, and spreading across the continent in the years to come (lukecommission.org). The founders, Dr. Harry and his wife (and physician's assistant) Echo VanderWal are the picture of what you would imagine medical missionaries to be. Their effectiveness rate has been noted by health organizations around the world, and is rooted in their dependence on God and sensitivity to the Swazi, and overall African, culture.

APPENDIX FOUR: THE TRANSFERABLIITY OF THE "GOD-SIZED VISION"

The "God-Sized Vision" at an urban Hispanic church

In the opening of this book, I mentioned that this template of Acts 1:8 can be translated to churches of any size. Indeed, CLC is a church of over 2,000 attendees, passionate about the God-Sized Vision. However, to support the idea that this can fit your church, below are two of my friends and partners in ministry, in front of their own version of the "God-Sized Vision Board."

Pastor Jesse, of Fuentes De Agua Viva in Dayton, pastors a Hispanic church with around 100 attendees (when we first partnered together, weekend attendance with about 50 people). He is shown below posing by his drawing.

The "God-Sized Vision" in Africa

Pastor Kevin Ward, of The Potter's Wheel Church in Mbabane, Swaziland, leads a church of about 600 in attendance (an overall congregation of over 1,200 people). Here he is "vision casting" the God-Sized Vision" for their church.

Connect with Stan:

I'm obviously a BIG believer in the "God-Sized Vision" approach to leading a church, as set out by Jesus in Acts 1:8. I've also seen how it has transformed our church and assisted other churches that have adopted it.

I realize that some of the principles can be challenging to implement and the task may seem daunting. If I can be of any assistance to you, please don't hesitate to contact me via email at: sjtharp1@gmail.com.

To the journey,

Stan Tharp, D. Min, M.B.A., M.A.

Cover photo taken by Stan Tharp in Hawane, Swaziland, Africa
Cover design by Jonathan Tharp

Made in the USA
Middletown, DE
24 January 2015